FLOWERS

ROSES

John F. Prevost
ABDO & Daughters

Published by Abdo & Daughters, 4940 Viking Drive, Suite 622, Edina, Minnesota 55435.

Copyright © 1996 by Abdo Consulting Group, Inc., Pentagon Tower, P.O. Box 36036, Minneapolis, Minnesota 55435 USA. International copyrights reserved in all countries. No part of this book may be reproduced in any form without written permission from the publisher.

Printed in the United States.

Cover Photo credits: Peter Arnold, Inc.
Interior Photo credits: Peter Arnold, Inc.

Edited by Bob Italia

Library of Congress Cataloging-in-Publication Data

Prevost, John F.
     Roses / John F. Prevost.
     p. cm. -- (Flowers)
     Includes index.
     Summary: Describes the variety of colors, various parts, growing conditions, and other aspects of one of the most popular flowers in the world.
     ISBN 1-56239-610-2
     1. Roses--Juvenile literature. [1. Roses.] I. Title. II. Series: Prevost, John F. Flowers
QK495.R78P74 1996
583' .372--dc20
                                                        95-49630
                                                         CIP
                                                         AC

Contents

Roses and Family

The most popular flowers grown in the world are roses. They are planted in gardens, in planters, and as **hedges**. Many are grown in **greenhouses** and inside homes. Roses are popular because of their beautiful colors, wonderful smell, and ability to **bloom** for a long time.

First raised in China 5,000 years ago, roses were popular flowers in ancient Europe, Asia, and Northern Africa. Today, roses are grown all over the world.

People have grown thousands of different **varieties** of these beautiful flowering plants. There are 284 wild rose varieties found in the Northern **Hemisphere**. Roses do not grow naturally in the Southern Hemisphere.

Opposite page: Roses are found all over the world.

Roots, Soil, and Water

Roses pull water from the soil with their roots. The roots also hold the roses upright and keep the plant from falling over.

Roses do not grow well in wet soil. Their roots will begin to rot and die. Roses do not like dry soil, either. Without enough water, the roots cannot keep the rest of the plant from drying out.

The soil must also have **minerals** and other **nutrients**, which the plant uses for food. Without enough food, roses will not grow or flower.

Roses need minerals and nutrients from the soil to grow and stay healthy.

Stems, Leaves, and Sunlight

The stems and leaves are the parts of the rose that grow in the sunlight. Sunlight is important to every green plant. It is used to change water, **nutrients,** and air into plant food. This process is called **photosynthesis.**

The stems hold up the leaves and allow them to collect sunlight. Stems send water from the roots to the leaves where food and **oxygen** are made. The food then returns to the roots.

Most rose plants have thorns to protect the stems from animals that want to eat them. Thornless roses, or smooth-stemmed roses, grow without thorns.

Photosynthesis

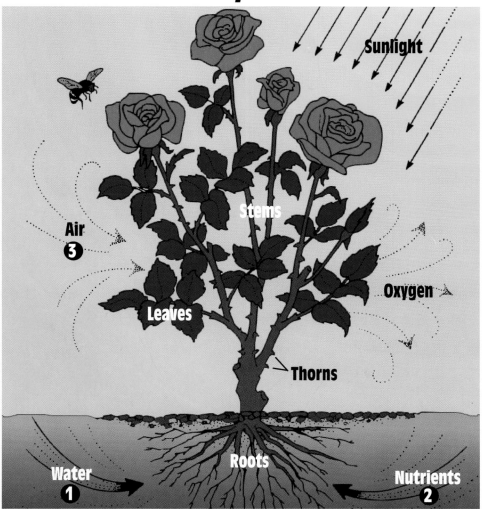

Ground water (1) and nutrients (2) travel through the roots and stems and into the leaves where air (3) is drawn in. Then the plant uses sunlight to change these three elements into food and oxygen.

Flowers

Rose plants are popular because of their flowers, which can be 1/2 to 7 inches (1 to 18 cm) across. Some roses do not have a scent, while others have strong scents. Rose flowers come in almost every color except black and blue.

Each flower has three main parts: the **petal,** the **stamen,** and the **pistil.** The petals are the showy part of the flower. These help us identify the different rose types. The stamen contains **pollen**, which **fertilizes** the flower. The pistil makes seeds.

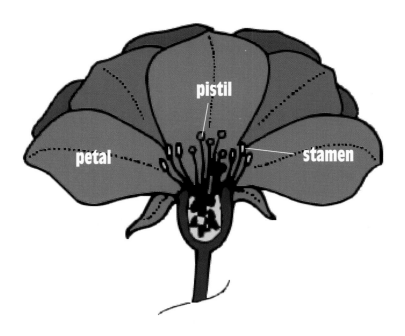

The three main parts of the rose flower: the petal, pistil, and stamen. The pistil and stamen help the rose reproduce.

Seeds

The seeds are found in the **rose hip.** The hip grows on the stem where the **petals** grew before falling off. Most people grow roses only for their flowers. But some are grown for the hips, which are made into jellies, preserves, and tea.

Seeds form when **pollen fertilizes ovules** inside the **pistil.** The ovules then grow into seeds that protect the plant **embryos** and the food inside. Rose seeds are **dormant** over the winter and sprout in the spring.

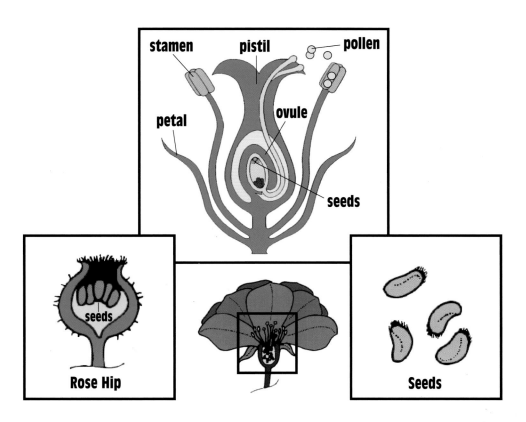

Pollen from the stamen fertilizes the pistil's ovules. The ovules grow into seeds, forming a rose hip. Inside each seed is a tiny plant embryo which will grow into a rose plant.

Insects and Other Friends

The rose plant uses its flowers to attract insects. The flowers' color and smell invite insects to land on the **blossom**. The flowers' sweet **nectar** rewards the insects with a small meal.

Bees, butterflies, moths, flies, hummingbirds, and small mice feed on the nectar. While feeding, **pollen** sticks to their legs. The animals spread the pollen when flying or crawling from flower to flower.

Some helpful insects like ladybugs and wasps live on the rose plant. These **predators** eat insect pests that chew on the plant. Spiders live on the leaves and stems. They also eat insect **pests.**

Bees help roses pollinate their flowers.

Pests and Diseases

Many plant-eating insects such as caterpillars eat roses. These chewing insect **pests** can kill the plant. They may be controlled with **predatory** insects or **poisonous** sprays.

Disease will attack weak or damaged plants. Sometimes insects spread diseases as they eat plants. **Chemicals** are often used to stop diseases.

Healthy rose plants can fight pests and diseases. Growing roses in the right location is important. Many **pure** roses are tougher than the **varieties**. Rose **breeders** are developing stronger roses.

Opposite page:
Water keeps roses healthy so they can fight pests and diseases.

Varieties

There are more than 30,000 rose **varieties** in the world. The American Rose Society lists 56 different **classes** of roses.

All **classification systems** separate the bush roses from the shrub roses, the climbing roses from the non-climbing, the older varieties from the newer varieties, and **pure** roses from **hybrids.**

The most popular class of roses are hybrid tea roses. The newest group of roses are the English roses. These combine the best of the old and new roses.

Opposite page:
Many pure roses are
tougher than the varieties.

Roses and the Plant Kingdom

The plant kingdom is divided into several groups, including flowering plants, fungi, plants with bare seeds, and ferns.

 Flowering plants grow flowers to make seeds. These seeds often grow inside protective ovaries or fruit.

 Fungi are plants without leaves, flowers, or green coloring, and cannot make their own food. They include mushrooms, molds, and yeast.

 Plants with bare seeds (such as evergreens and conifers) do not grow flowers. Their seeds grow unprotected, often on the scale of a cone.

 Ferns are plants with roots, stems, and leaves. They do not grow flowers or seeds.

There are two groups of flowering plants: monocots (MAH-no-cots) and dicots (DIE-cots). Monocots have seedlings with one leaf. Dicots have seedlings with two leaves.

The rose family is one type of dicot. All rose varieties and some fruit trees—including apple trees—are part of the rose family.

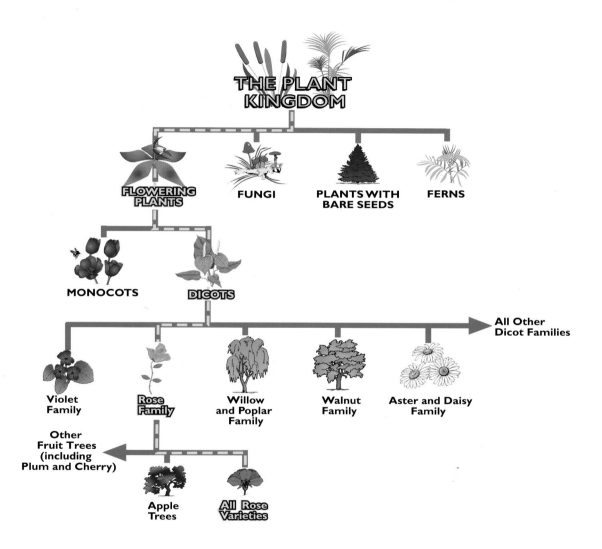

THE PLANT KINGDOM

FLOWERING PLANTS

FUNGI

PLANTS WITH BARE SEEDS

FERNS

MONOCOTS

DICOTS

All Other Dicot Families

Violet Family

Rose Family

Willow and Poplar Family

Walnut Family

Aster and Daisy Family

Other Fruit Trees (including Plum and Cherry)

Apple Trees

All Rose Varieties

21

Glossary

bloom - To have flowers; also, a flower blossom.

blossom (BLAH-sum) - The flower of a plant.

breeder (BREE-der) - A person who reproduces plants.

chemicals (KEM-ih-kulls) - A substance used to create a reaction or process.

classes - A grouping of similar plants.

classification system - A way of grouping living things.

disease (diz-EEZ) - A sickness.

dormant (DOOR-mant) - The state of rest or inactivity.

embryo (EM-bree-oh) - An early stage of plant growth, before sprouting from a seed.

fertilize (FUR-tuh-lies) - To develop the ovule into a seed.

greenhouse - A building made for growing plants.

hedge - A row of bushes that form a wall.

hemisphere (HEM-iss-fear) - Half of the earth's surface. The Northern Hemisphere is north of the equator and the Southern Hemisphere is south of the equator.

hybrid (HI-brid) - The offspring of two different plants.

mineral - Any substance that is not a plant, animal, or another living thing.

nectar - A sweet fluid found in some flowers.

nutrients (NEW-tree-ents) - Substances that help a plant grow and stay healthy.

ovule (AH-vule) - A seed before it is fertilized by pollen.

oxygen (OX-ih-jen) - A gas without color, taste, or odor found in air and water.

pest- A harmful or destructive insect.

petal (PET-ull) - One of several leaves that protect the center of a flower.

photosynthesis (foe-toe-SIN-thuh-sis) - The use of sunlight to make food.

pistil (PIS-till) - The female (seed-making) flower part.

poison - A substance that is dangerous to life or health.

pollen - A yellow powder that fertilizes flowers.

pollinate (PAHL-ih-nate) - The use of pollen to fertilize a flower.

predator (PRED-uh-tore) - An animal that eats other animals.

pure - A flower that grows naturally in the wild.

rose hip - The part of the stem where the petals grow before falling off.

stamen (STAY-men) - The male flower part (the flower part that makes pollen).

varieties (vuh-RYE-uh-tees) - Different types of plants that are closely related.

Index

583
PRE

Prevost, John F.

Roses

DATE DUE	BORROWER'S NAME	ROOM NUMBER
4/28/9?	Jhoana Salas	47
1/20/98	Hay Horm	51

583
PRE

Prevost, John F.

Roses